Index

What to serve • and how to serve it

by JOSEPH S. EDELMAN

THE passing of prohibition brings back the old half-forgotten problem of what to serve—and how to serve it. Many erudite volumes have been written on the subject and many experts have crossed swords (verbally, of course) on behalf of this or that in relation to wines and liqueurs, but most of them are fairly in agreement on a few of the simpler problems. In this little booklet I have tried to put all this terrifying accumulation of knowledge into simple, understandable and not too complicated verbiage.

Experts may talk as learnedly as they please of vintages and of the hair splitting differences between one wine and another. Keep before you the few simple facts that experience has taught us jibe with good common sense and for the rest let your own judgment and preferences rule.

You will find many a wine that boasts of no vintage year that will please your palate as well as the more expensive types that rate high on the experts' charts.

You may like a sweeter wine when the more knowing prefer a dry—For your every day table you may prefer a vin ordinaire that you will relish as much as the expert does his "premier cru".

Experiment for yourself and let your own preference guide you to your personal choice.

One interesting book on the "Art of Wining and Dining with Rhyme and Reason" gives this sensible advice: "order, for example, a case of white wines, and ask your vintner to make each bottle a different kind in brand, year and even grade. Then make a few notes on each bottle as you open it and by the end of six months or so, you'll begin to realize that you have tastes to develop."

Now that's sensible advice indeed.

After all, the rules of intelligent service and the proper care of wines and liquors are not too involved for anyone to understand.

And it is in that spirit that we bring you this little booklet, with our sincere hope that you will find it of real help.

In Buying Wines

Keep in mind that the safest way to buy wines is from a reputable dealer whom you can depend upon.

Check the labels of your wines to make sure that the bottle bears in addition to the name of the wine, the name of a wine importer or distributor of standing.

In Serving Wines

A few simple rules should be remembered.

White wines should be chilled or iced. Red wines should be served at approximately room temperatures. Bring the red wines up from the cellar and place them in the room where they are to be served several hours before service.

Chill the white wines in the ice box for a few hours before service. Champagne and very sweet white wines should be thoroughly iced before serving.

Never serve a red wine before a white or a red Burgundy before a claret or a sweet wine before a dry one. Because dry wines are more delicate in flavor, the more robust vintages kill their taste.

In Keeping Wines

You need observe but a few simple precautions.

If you live in an apartment, a dry closet can be arranged for your wine storeroom and kept at satisfactory temperature by lining it with insulation board.

If you own a home of your own you can easily fix up a wine cellar, preferably underground. Remember not to store them where they will freeze, or too near a furnace where the heat will hasten fermentation. A uniform temperature of approximately fifty-five degrees Fahrenheit is the ideal to strive for. A small room, partitioned off with hollow tile or insulation material of some sort, in a spot that will be dark, dry and well ventilated, will serve the purpose well. Build shelves into this compartment so that you place each type of wine or liquor in the manner best suited to its needs. Place your bottles so that you can remove the top ones without disturbing the others. Keep each variety by itself if possible.

Place the bottles upon their sides so that the cork remains wet and wedge them in to prevent rolling.

Ports, Sherries and Madeiras should stand upright. Brandies, gins and whiskies should also remain upright. If you buy wines in a case, turn it on its side so that the corks are kept moist and you can then remove the bottles from the top without disturbing those remaining.

What Wines to Serve

Serving the proper wine with the proper food is not merely a ceremonial. It has sound reason behind it. By choosing the correct wines for various foods you enhance the flavor and enjoyment of both the food and the wine and aid the digestion as well.

For a party dinner you may serve several wines for various courses. When you serve one wine with the family dinner, choose it to accompany the main dish.

A simple rule to follow is this—serve red wines with red meats and white wines with white meats and light repasts.

For a not too elaborate dinner you may serve a sherry before the meal for an appetizer—a dry wine during the meal and a sweet wine as a liqueur with the dessert or after it. You can, if you wish, serve a sherry during the dinner if you prefer it.

WITH OYSTERS

Serve a dry wine such as Chablis, Dry Sherry or White Capri.

WITH THE SOUP
Serve a sherry, Madeira or Moselle.

WITH FISH

A semi-dry white wine, Moselle, White Graves, light Burgundy, Reisling or Sauterne.

WITH ENTREES

For sweetbreads, creamed lobster, chicken, guinea hen, light meats or light game, curried dishes or quail use a light red wine, claret, or a white wine, Burgundy, Montrachet, Meursault or Hermitage. With chicken or turkey you can also serve dry white wines such as Chablis, Riesling or Sauterne.

WITH RED MEATS OR GAME

Use a dry red wine such as Plume, Burgundy, Claret or Chianti.

WITH DESSERTS

Such as pastries, fruit or cheese, serve Haut Sauternes or Champagne, Madeira, Malmsey, Marsala or Muscatel.

AFTER DINNER

As liqueurs, serve port, Madeira, Sherry, Malaga, Tokay, Angelica or Muscatel. Salted nuts, crackers and cheese may be served when several wines are used so that the taste of each wine may be neutralized in preparation for the one to follow.

Testing Wines

A simple way for the average man to judge a wine is to give it a simple test—what wine men call the eye, nose and mouth tests.

Use a crystal clear glass which does not alter the color of the wine. Fill your glass only half full, or only a third full if the glass is large. Hold the glass to the light. See if the wine is clear and transparent—free from sediment or muddiness. Note the color, the transparency, and clarity.

Before you taste it, rotate the glass gently to release the aroma and bouquet of the wine. Pass the glass under your nose so that you can smell the characteristic odor of the wine. If it smells clean, fragrant, fruity, it is a good wine. If it has a musty, mousy, vinegary smell, it is not a good wine.

Taste the wine by taking a thimbleful or so and swish it around with your tongue and on the roof of your mouth. Let your palate tell you if the taste is clean and pleasant.

Swallow the wine slowly. See if the after taste is clean, smooth and velvety. You need not be an expert to know if a wine pleases you by these tests.

Cooking with Wines

Mrs. Margaret Francis in an introduction to her book of recipes entitled "Cooking with Wines," says:

"The perfection of cooking as attained by the French and Latins generally, and later adopted by the Teutons, is only possible with the use of wines. The crude makeshift of vinegar, used almost entirely by the English speaking people, accounts for the paucity of real good, palatable and satisfying dishes in England and America, excepting where wine is used in some form as in English plum pudding and American mince pie, or the famous terrapin stew a la Maryland."

The use of wine adds much to the palatability of the following dishes:

SOUP.—A cup of white wine, added a few minutes before soups are ready to serve greatly improves the flavor. Sherry, Madeira or similar wines are generally used for soups made principally of meat and fish stock, and Moselle, Sauterne or Rhine Wine is used for soups with a vegetable stock like pea, bean, etc.

FISH.—Fish served in the French way in shells, with a dressing that contains a liberal flavoring of white wine, is a real delicacy. The cheaper kinds of fish cooked with a wine sauce are both palatable and wholesome. The famous filet of sole a la Marquery is made with Sherry; and oysters steamed in wine are delicious.

SAUCES—The French and other Latin races always use wine in their sauces and gravies. The brown stock that is the basis of all dark sauces is either Sherry or Madeira, and the white stock for light sauces also has some one of the white wines as an ingredient. The famous sauce Bordelaise contains red wine and sauce Hollandaise has white wine.

STEWS AND ROASTS—The Europeans generally use the cheaper cuts of meat for stews and they always contain some wine. The celebrated Goulash, for instance, should contain both a white wine and a Madeira or similar wine to give it the rich flavor that was developed by its inventors, the Hungarians. The French pot roast would be incomplete without a liberal flavoring of red wine, and chicken fricassee, if properly prepared, contains both white wine and a little sweet wine like Catawba. The famous champagne sauce for baked ham is not a name only, but is actually made with champagne, and the cheaper brands of American wine are better suited for this purpose than the more expensive French "bruts."

VEGETABLES—Italian spaghetti has either white or red wine in the sauce. Rice, Italian style, is rendered more appetizing by the use of some white wine. The famous German sauerkraut always has white wine, and even Champagne is used in cooking this dish.

DESSERTS—Foreign chefs use wine liberally in their puddings and pastry. Many of the best cakes contain sweet wines like Angelica or Muscatel, while the famous Baba a la rhum (rum) is considered a delicacy in every land. There are many kinds of wine jellies, and sauces for puddings are generally flavored with wine.

TYPES OF WINES AND THEIR USES

Natural Wines

The light wines produced by a process of natural fermentation come under this classification. They are usually the product of one vineyard and after a short period of active fermentation are stored for several years and then bottled.

RED BORDEAUX

Are dry clarets, light in flavor and body. They are excellent table wines for service throughout the meal. May be used to accompany the entree or the roast. Should be served at room temperatures. The most famous are wines that are chateau labeled and bottled.

WHITE BORDEAUX

These wines include both dry and sweet wines. They have a light, delicate flavor and bouquet which is very distinctive. The dry wines known as Graves are usually served with the fish course. The Sauterne which is a sweet wine, and the Barsacs, are usually served as dessert wines. Should be served cooled.

RED BURGANDIES (France)

Is a wine of rich flavor and heavy body, known as the "Wine of Kings." It is served with red meats and roasts. Service should be at room temperature. Care should be exercised in serving not to stir up the sediment in the bottle.

WHITE BURGUNDIES

These are extremely dry wines usually served with the fish course. Served chilled about 20 degrees below room temperature.

RHINE WHITE WINES (France and Germany)

Fruity wines, dry and light, usually served with fish courses.

RHONE WINES (France)

Are found in both red and white types. Served in the same manner as Burgundies, and with the same characteristics, but a trifle drier.

CHIANTI (Italy)

Both red and white types. The red type runs from dry to slightly sweet. The white is semi-dry. Use the white wines with fish—the red wines with entrees or meats. Serve cooled to 20 degrees below room temperatures.

Fortified Wines

As a rule fortified wines are sweet. They are produced from wines of different vineyards, blended and naturally fermented. Before fermentation is completed, a proportion of grape brandy is added.

It is aged in the wood and this aging process is completed after bottling to give it added bouquet and mellowness.

PORT (RED and tawny)

Is a rich and full bodied wine, heavy and sweet in flavor and with rich mineral content. It has a delicate and distinctive bouquet and is served with fruit and nuts as a dessert wine. Serve at room temperature.

SHERRY (Spain)

This amber wine is Spain's most important wine product. It is a semi-sweet wine with a nutty, aromatic, elusive flavor. The Amontillado is the finest dry type. Oloroso is the finest of the sweet types. Dry types should be served before meals as an appetizer or with soup. Semi-sweet types may be used as a wine with meals. Sweet types should be served with desserts. Serve at room temperature.

TOKAY (Hungary)

A light, delicate amber wine with a distinctive flavor, served with the dessert at room temperature.

MUSCATEL (Italy)

A fairly sweet wine, rich in body with a fine fruity flavor. Used as a dessert wine and served at room temperature.

MADEIRA (Portugal)

A light and delicate wine with more body than the natural white wines. Similar to Tokay but drier, it is a good dessert wine. Serve at room temperature.

MALAGA (Spain)

Although it resembles sherry, it is much sweeter and lacks the nuttiness of its drier compatriot. A good dessert wine, served at room temperature.

Sparkling Wines

Of the Chablis and Moselle Types, are similar to dry champagne. The sparkle is usually the result of artificial carbonization. They are very dry wines, served with the fish course. Should be thoroughly chilled before serving. The Burgundy type is richer and sweeter, served with roast or game, and also used as a dessert wine. Serve well chilled.

CHAMPAGNE (France)

The important wine that graces every special occasion. Has a light, golden color, a delicate, pleasant, tingly taste and a bubbling effervescence. Types are Doux (very sweet), Sec (Dry), Extra Dry, Brut (very dry). The dry types may be served with fish courses. The sweet types with dessert. Serve thoroughly iced.

American Wines

Not all the fine wines come from European countries. Our own Eastern states and California produce many wines of fine quality and flavor. Many are similar in type to European wines and others are distinctly American types. Like European countries, America produces wines of every shade of quality. After all, the favorite wine is a matter of personal preference and experience will quickly teach you which wines you personally prefer. California produces many interesting varieties—about 80% of our wines come from this area.

FROM RUTHERFORD, CAL. Dry red and white wines of the Sauterne, Chablis, and Sherry types are popular.

SAN FRANCISCO. Chianti, Claret, Sherry, Muscatel and Port types and excellent white wines of various French and German types, including Champagnes.

SAN JOSE. Various still dry and sweet wines.

ASTI, CAL. Chianti types.

GUASTI, CAL. Sweet and dry wines. Sherries and Port types.

KINGSBURY, CAL. Wines of several types.

LODI, CAL. Sherry and Port wines.

Among well-known Eastern wines are the Champagnes made in St. Louis, the Ports, Burgundies, Clarets and Champagne types made in Egg Harbor, N. J. The wines bearing purely American names, like Virginia Dare and Paul Garrett Champagnes, made in Brooklyn, the Tokay and Port types made in Naples, New York, Champagne from Rheims, N. Y., and Urbana and still red and white wines made in Naples, N. Y.

POL BONNET—An imported French
MARCEL LORAIN—Imported Frenc
MIRAMONT SEC (GOLDEN—One c
MIRAMONT SEC (BURGUNDY)—R∈
SPANISH BURGUNDY (SPARKLING
SPANISH BURGUNDY—Red. Finest
SPANISH SHERRY—Golden. A rich
SPANISH MALAGA—Golden. Fine
SPANISH PORT—Red. Rich, full boc
SPANISH CHABLIS (SPARKLING)—
SPANISH CHABLIS—White. Very fi

FINE WINES AT A SENSIBLE PRICE —

ne with a 150 year reputation.
agne, nothing finer produced.
st of domestic Champagne wines.
of the finest sparkling domestic wines.
A fine, sparkling imported wine.
mported still wine.
vine for everyday use.
ported wine for every taste.
rful imported wine.
right, sparkling imported wine.
imported still wine.

TY AND VALUE IN GREATEST MEASURE

The Story of Champagne

Champagne comes from the champagne district of France, whose boundaries are set by French Law. Only wine grown from grapes in this limited area may be termed "champagne."

It is the "wine of ceremony," made with meticulous care from the black grapes of the best vineyards. White grapes are added to some fine blends in varying quantities to impart a subtle bouquet and rare distinction.

At grape gathering time, usually toward the end of September, the precious bunches are carefully picked, placed in small baskets, and inspected one by one on wicker picking trays. They are then placed in large baskets containing 130 to 220 pounds and delivered to the presses of the purchasing merchants or their agents together with the indication of the vineyard owner.

Large surface presses, peculiar to the champagne district, are used to separate the juice as soon as the fruit is crushed. Each press contains four tons of grapes. The first juice which flows yields 440 gallons or ten champagne barrels of first pressing wine.

Under the influence of natural fermentation the sugar in the grape is transformed into alcohol which remains in solution, and into carbonic gas. In high class wines the temperature of fermentation is kept low in order that the "bouquet" of the best vintages may attain its maximum delicacy.

In December, under the influence of cold, fermentation ceases, the lees fall to the bottom of the cask and the wine becomes clear. It is then drawn off and wines of similar origin are assembled. These wines are placed in casks, hermetically sealed.

The wine is blended by mixing of the various lots in large vats. It is then clarified by means of very fine sturgeon isinglass; at the end of April the wine is ready to be placed in the cellars if intended for the reserves or to be bottled.

The bottles have a capacity of about one quart. The glass is of uniform thickness to resist the enormous pressure.

Bottling commences at the end of April when the Spring brings on a second fermentation. At this period the wine is carefully tested to ascertain the exact quanity of sugar. This operation is regulated, and then the bottles are stoppered with a special cork to keep it hermetically sealed in the cellar for years. This "drawing" cork is kept in place by a special clip. The bottles are stacked in the cellars and the contents undergo a process of slow fermentation.

After some months the wine has become frothy. Its position is changed several times in the course of two or three years. When it has reached maturity the deposit of ferments has settled to the bottom of the bottle. By long and delicate manipulation on perforated tables inclined at steep angles, this sediment is collected on the cork of the bottle. Each day, in order to detach the sediment, each bottle in the rack is subjected to slight jerks and rotations. These delicate daily movements last from four to six months.

Finally, when the bottle is almost vertical, the sediment has gathered on the cork—the wine is as clear as crystal. The bottle is then said to be "finished on end." It is then set up vertically "en masse," neck downward.

The sediment is removed by uncorking the bottle. By a clever knock the cork is sprung and the sediment resting on it comes with it. The crystal clear wine alone remains. When the bottle has been cleared, a certain proportion of the wine is replaced by a liquor composed of absolutely pure cane sugar dissolved in wine of high quality.

If no cane sugar liquid is added it is a "natural" champagne. If about 2% sugar is added it is called "Extra Dry." 4 to 5% of sugar is known as "American flavor." From 6% to 7% is known as "Dry," from 7% to 10% "Half Dry." More than that is known as "Sweet."

The bottle is at last ready to receive its final cork before being shipped. The cork is forced in by a powerful machine. It is kept in place by a wire muzzle. The bottle is kept on its side in order to ensure the preservation of the cork and that of the froth.

The discovery of champagne was made by Don Perignon, a Benedictine Monk, of the 17th Century, who called it the "Wine of Stars."

Delicacy, lightness, subtle and lasting sparkle distinguish champagnes—the King of Beverages.

Cordials and Liqueurs

Used for appetizers and after dinner liquers. They vary widely in taste and character according to their origin and are usually served in small quantities. Among the best known are:

BENEDICTINE
A liquid of deep golden color originally created by the monks of the Benedictine Abbey of Fecamp.

CHARTREUSE
Which is made in three different types and colors —white, yellow and green. This is another of the liquers prepared by the busy monks.

CREME DE MENTHE
A green, sweet liqueur flavored with mint leaves.

CURACAO
A liqueur created from orange peel and alcohol to which sugar syrup has been added after distillation. Holland produces the best grades, usually white or yellow with strong orange bitter flavor.

Distilled Liquors

Owe their different characters to the difference in the materials employed in their making and the varying methods applied.

Here in a few brief words are the differences.

BRANDY

Is produced from a wine or blend of wines distilled into a liquor of higher alcoholic content. The finest brandy comes from the town of Cognac in France and bears that name. Good brandy has a fine smooth taste, flavor and aroma, acquired from several years of aging.

GIN

Is distilled from rye or barley flavored by the addition of juniper berries during rectification. Holland originated it, but English distillers produce it widely. "London Gin" is a colorless liquid of fine flavor.

RUM

Is an ardent spirit distilled from molasses or cane sugar. It is generally pale yellow to dark amber in color. One of the best known is Bacardi Rum, produced in Cuba.

WHISKEY

Is distilled spirit from malt, rye or a mixture of rye or barley malt and unmalted rye. The Bourbon is made from barley malt or a mixture of wheat, malt, and corn.

ANISETTE

Is distilled from green anise seed, star anise, and coriander seed, sweetened and enriched with orange flower water. White in color.

KIRSCHWASSER

Made from cherries.

KÜMMEL

Distilled from alcohol and caraway seed and sweetened. White in color.

COINTREAU

White in color and flavored with orange.

CREME DE CACAO

Made from an infusion of cocoa, alcohol and sugar syrup.

BRANDIES

Distilled from peaches, cherries, apricots, prunes, sweetened and colored. Have each the characteristic flavor of the fruit from which it was prepared.

VERMOUTH

An alcoholic wine flavored with various ingredients used both as a liquor and cocktail flavoring.

Some Popular Cocktails

AFFINITY COCKTAIL

1/3 French Vermouth, 1/3 Italian Vermouth, 1/3 Scotch, 2 dashes angostura bitters. Stir and strain into cocktail glass. Serve with lemon peel.

BACARDI COCKTAIL

1/2 jigger Italian Vermouth, 3/4 jigger Bacardi rum, dash of pineapple syrup. Shake well with cracked ice until very cold. A half teaspoon of lime juice and a half teaspoon plain syrup may be used instead of the pineapple syrup.

BRANDY COCKTAIL

2 portions brandy, 1 portion orange juice, 1/2 portion lemon juice, 1 teaspoon sugar, 2 dashes orange bitters.

BRANDY FIZZ

Cordial glass brandy, juice of 1 lemon, teaspoon sugar, 2 dashes Benedictine, or yellow Chartreuse. Shake well and fill with charged water.

BRANDY FLIP

1 wine glass brandy, 1 teaspoon sugar syrup, 1 fresh egg, 2 lumps ice. Shake thoroughly, strain, and add a little nutmeg on top before serving.

BRANDY HIGHBALL

Cordial glass brandy. Fill glass with charged water. Serve with or without ice.

BRANDY PUNCH

I teaspoon sugar dissolved in a little water. I teaspoon pineapple syrup, I wineglass brandy, juice of half a lemon, 1/2 glass rum. Add shaved ice, shake thoroughly and decorate top with fruits in season or from a can and serve with a straw.

BRANDY SMASH

Crush small lump of sugar and a few sprigs of mint in old fashioned whiskey glass and add cordial glass of brandy. Add cracked ice, stir and serve.

BRONX

1/2 jigger gin, 1/2 jigger French Vermouth, I teaspoon orange juice. Mix in tall glass with cracked ice until thoroughly chilled and strain into cocktail glasses.

CHAMPAGNE COCKTAIL

I piece of lemon peel in tall glass, fill glass with shaved ice, fill to brim with champagne, add dash orange bitters and stir.

CHAMPAGNE CUP

In a glass pitcher add a cordial glass of cognac or brandy to a cordial glass of maraschino, a cordial glass of creme de menthe or Chartreuse, a cordial glass of syrup or tablespoon sugar, juice of I lemon, and I orange. Mix with ice and a pint of cold sparkling water and a quart of cold champagne. To add color, drop in several slices of lemon, orange, pineapple, and a few cherries and sprigs of mint.

Jigger : a graded measuring glass

CHAMPAGNE PUNCH

To one quart of white Vin Ordinaire add 1 pint curacao, chartreuse, or other liqueur; 1 cup of brandy, 1 pint of lemon juice, 1 sliced orange, 3 sliced limes, 1/4 box strawberries hulled and halved. Sugar to taste. Mix well and chill in icebox. Strain into punch bowl with large cake of ice. Add 2 quarts cold champagne, 1 quart of sparkling water. Dress with strawberries,, cherries and grapes.

CLARET PUNCH

2 jigge.s of claret, 1 spoon sugar, juice of 1 lemon. Pour into shaker with ice. Add several pieces of pineapple and orange in goblet.

CLOVER CLUB COCKTAIL

4 parts gin, juice of 1 lime, white of 1 egg, 1 part Italian Vermouth, 1 part Grenadine. Add ice and shake well.

CLOVER LEAF

1 jigger gin, 1/2 tablespoon Grenadine syrup, 2 tablespoons cream. Shake well with cracked ice and strain into cocktail glasses.

SHERRY FLIP

Yolk of an egg, 1 teaspoon sugar, 1 glass of Sherry, shake well with ice, strain, and spread with nutmeg.

CLUB COCKTAIL

In a mixing glass add 2 dashes orange bitters, 2 dashes yellow Chartreuse, 2 dashes French Vermouth, 1 jigger gin. Pour into shaker with ice. Frappe. Strain into cocktail glass. Serve with piece of lemon peel.

DUBONNET

1/2 jigger dry gin, 1/2 jigger Dubonnet, dash orange bitter. Mix by stirring with cracked ice until thoroughly chilled. Strain into cocktail glasses.

DUBONNET FIZZ

To juice of half an orange, add juice of half a lemon, 1 teaspoon Cherry Brandy, 1 glass Dubonnet. Add ice and shake.

GIN HIGHBALL

In a highball glass, place piece of ice, 1 piece of lemon peel, jigger of gin. Fill glass with seltzer. Serve with small spoon.

GIN RICKEY

In a rickey glass place a piece of ice. Add 1 jigger gin, juice of 1/2 lime. Fill with seltzer and serve with small spoon.

GIN SOUR

1 teaspoon sugar syrup, 3 dashes of lemon juice, 1 wineglass gin, a little seltzer. Add shaved ice, shake, and strain. Dress top with orange.

HORSE'S NECK

Place in large Tom Collins glass 2 pieces of ice, rind of one lemon, jigger gin, I bottle ginger ale, and add teaspoon sugar. Stir and serve.

JACK ROSE COCKTAIL

4 parts Apple jack, 2 parts gin, I part French Vermouth, I part Italian Vermouth, 2 parts orange juice, 2 parts lime or lemon juice, enough Grenadine to color. Add ice if preferred.

JOHN COLLINS

I wineglass gin, I teaspoon sugar syrup, juice of $\frac{1}{2}$ lemon, add ice and fill with seltzer.

MANHATTAN

$\frac{2}{3}$ jigger Bourbon whiskey, $\frac{1}{3}$ jigger Italian vermouth, dash Angostura bitters. Stir (do not shake) in tall glass with cracked ice until thoroughly chilled and strain into cocktail glasses.

For dry Manhattan, use French instead of Italian Vermouth.

MARTINI COCKTAIL (Dry)

In a shaker put I part French Vermouth, I part gin. Shake well with chipped ice and put an olive in each glass.

MARTINI COCKTAIL (Sweet)

I part gin, I part Italian Vermouth, I dash sugar syrup. Add ice, shake well.

NEW ORLEANS GIN FIZZ

1 white of egg, 1 teaspoon sugar, 1 small glass gin, juice of 1 lemon, ice, $\frac{1}{2}$ wineglass fresh cream. Shake well, strain to a glass and dilute with seltzer.

NIGHT CAP

To the yolk of a fresh egg, add 1 part Anisette, 1 part Curacao, 1 part brandy. Chill, shake well, strain and serve.

OLD FASHIONED COCKTAIL

One lump of sugar on which a dash of orange or Angostura bitters has been squirted. 1 jigger of any kind of whiskey desired, and dress with a piece of twisted lemon or orange peel. Mix in old fashioned cocktail glass.

ORANGE BLOSSOM

Juice of $\frac{1}{2}$ orange and $\frac{1}{4}$ lemon, 1 jigger gin, two tablespoons orange ice. Shake well, pour into glasses and top with seltzer water.

ROCK AND RYE

1 wineglass rye, 1 teaspoon rock-candy syrup or sugar syrup, juice of half a lemon. Stir thoroughly and serve.

SHERRY COBBLER

In a large glass put lots of ice. Add 1 part brandy, 1 part Curacao, 1 part Maraschino, 2 parts Sherry, a few slices of fresh fruit and sprinkle with Port wine.

SIDE CAR

Rim top of cocktail glass with orange and dip in powdered sugar. Mix juice of half a lemon with I teaspoon powdered sugar, $\frac{1}{2}$ jigger brandy, $\frac{1}{2}$ jigger Cointreau. Mix as for Manhattan.

SILVER FIZZ

I wineglass gin, 3 small lumps of ice, white of I egg, juice of half lemon or lime, I tablespoon sugar, shake thoroughly and strain, then fill with seltzer.

SLOEGIN FIZZ

In a mixing glass place I jigger sloe gin. Add spoon sugar, dash lemon juice. Pour into shaker with ice. Frappe. Strain into fizz glass and add a little seltzer.

STINGER

$\frac{1}{2}$ jigger Creme de Menthe, I jigger brandy. Mix as for Manhattan.

TOM AND JERRY

Put yolk of one egg in one bowl and white in another. Beat each thoroughly. Then mix together. Add a spoonful of powdered sugar. Put a spoonful of the mixture in a glass and add I jigger brandy, $\frac{1}{2}$ jigger of rum. Fill with hot milk or water. Add a little nutmeg and serve.

TOM COLLINS

I wineglass gin, juice of one lemon, I teaspoon sugar syrup. Add ice and shake well, strain and fill with seltzer.

Liqueur   Red Wine   Sparkling Burgundy   Sherry

Glassware

Certain shapes for certain uses have become a matter of tradition—yet there is reason behind it all. The proper glassware adds to the interest and savor of a wine or liquor. There is a personal choice between similar types and here you may use your own discretion. We have suggested here the most popular shapes available for various purposes.

Never serve wine in highly colored goblets, cups or large glasses. Thin glasses, colorless and transparent are a rule you can profit by.

We illustrate here a wide variety of glassware for those who are sticklers for form and variety. For those who do not require too elaborate a service, we suggest a set of cocktail glasses, wine glasses, highball glasses, cordial glasses and beer mugs as ample for most families.

Water Goblet   **Brandy Inhaler**   **Champagne**

Old Fashioned   **Cocktail**   **Whiskey & Soda**   **White Wine**

Glassware arranged by MACY'S